VISION BOARD

CLIP ART BOOK

JUST A FRIENDLY REMINDER

This book serves as a guide and is not intended to substitute professional advice. Neither the author nor the publisher can be held responsible for any loss or damage that may arise from using or misusing the book or its contents. If you have any health concerns, it's always a good idea to consult with your physician. They're the experts who can provide the best guidance for your specific needs. Your well-being is important, so make sure to seek medical supervision for any health-related matters.

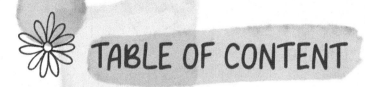

TABLE OF CONTENT

MANIFEST YOUR DREAMS

Are you ready to turn your aspirations into reality in the upcoming year?

Let's create a **vision board** that will serve as your compass, guiding you toward your dreams and goals. By regularly seeing these visual representations of your goals, you will be more motivated and inspired to work toward achieving them.

WHAT IS A VISION BOARD?

A Vision Board is a visual representation of one's **goals, dreams,** and **aspirations**. It typically consists of a collage of images, words, and phrases that depict what a person wants to achieve or manifest in life.

Vision boards help you clarify your goals, stay motivated, and maintain focus on your desired outcomes.

THE BENEFITS OF A VISION BOARD

- **Clarity and Focus:** It hones your focus, defining and clarifying goals to align your efforts with your desires.
- **Motivation and Inspiration:** It serves as a daily reminder of your dreams, driving motivation to act and progress toward your goals.
- **Positive Mindset:** Regular engagement with your vision board cultivates a positive mindset, replacing doubt with belief and transforming obstacles into opportunities.
- **Goal Success:** Studies suggest that vision board creators are likely to achieve their goals and dreams.
- **Visualization:** A vision board aids in visualization, helping you manifest your desires through the law of attraction.

MATERIALS

- A board (e.g., corkboard, foam board, poster board, or digital canvas).
- Scissors for cutting out images and words.
- Glue or adhesive for attaching cutouts to the board.
- Markers or colored pencils for adding personal touches and decorations.

HOW TO USE

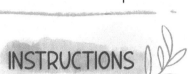

INSTRUCTIONS

Step 1: Set Your Intentions
Be specific about your intentions and goals in various life areas, such as career, relationships, health, and personal growth.

Step 2: Gather and Cut Out
Collect images, words, and phrases from this book and other sources that represent your aspirations.

Step 3: Arrange Your Materials
Organize the materials you've collected into categories or themes based on your goals.

Step 4: Create Your Vision Board
Begin by arranging your images, words, and phrases on a board in a manner that is visually appealing and meaningful to you. Be creative and follow your intuition.

Step 5: Personalize
Add your unique touch with drawings, colors, decorations, affirmations, or personal messages.

Step 6: Visualize
Take a few moments each day to visualize your goals. Use your vision board as a source of inspiration and motivation to take action toward your aspirations.

LOOK BACK AT 2024

1. What went well in 2024?

_____

_____

_____

2. What goals did you fall short on? Why?

_____

_____

_____

3. What was the single most challenging thing that happened?

_____

_____

_____

4. What have you learned from both your successes and failures?

_____

_____

_____

5. Give 2024 a name before saying goodbye.

2024 WAS THE YEAR OF _____

 Okay, now it's time to set your sights on the year ahead!

2025 REFLECTION QUESTIONS

1. How do you envision an extraordinary 2025? What S.M.A.R.T. goals will you set for 2025?

_____

_____

_____

_____

2. What personal qualities or skills would you like to develop in 2025?

_____

_____

3. How do you nurture your relationships with loved ones this year

_____

_____

4. What new knowledge or skills would you be interested in learning this year?

_____

_____

5. What will you do to improve your physical health?

_____

_____

6. What are your long-term financial goals?

_____

_____

7. What would be a fitting title for the story of 2025?

2025 WILL BE THE YEAR OF _____

Let's illuminate the path leading to 2025!

A GENTLE REMINDER

A well-crafted vision board serves as a beacon of inspiration and motivation, reminding you of your deepest desires. Regularly revisiting your board can fuel your drive to achieve them.

However, challenges are inevitable. You might encounter frustration with slow progress or feel overwhelmed by the constant visual nudges. These emotions are perfectly normal and shared by many.

The key lies in maintaining a balanced perspective when creating your vision board. While it's a powerful tool for focus and motivation, remember that success often comes hand-in-hand with challenges. Adapting your goals and strategies along the way is a natural part of the process.

Think of your vision board as a glimpse of your future destination, but savor the journey. Embrace resilience and celebrate your progress, no matter how small.

Slay The Day

Love Yourself

I CAN DO IT

CHASE YOUR
DREAMS

Every moment
MATTERS

SMILE
and be
HAPPY

UNSTOPPABLE

Passion Enjoy

Confidence

BE
STRONG

Trust

Improve Hope

BALANCE

Good Vibes

POSITIVE MIND

Great Life

Do all things
with
KINDNESS

Grateful

Blessed   Thankful

Meditation

Just Breath

Relax

THINK POSITIVE

Make It
Different

Hobbies

Creativity

GYM

Yoga

Running **Exercise**

WORKOUT

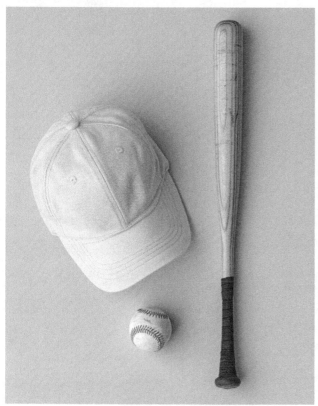

SPORTS
Health
KEEP FIGHTING

Sleep well

Self-care

Healthy Hair

EAT LESS SUGAR
You're sweet enough

DRINK MORE WATER

Reach my goal weight

Eat more **vegetables**

Healthy Food

LƟVE

Soulmate

Dating

Romantic

Together Forever   Married

Wedding   Happiness

Super Mom

Family

Home

family

where life begins
and love never ends

Quality Time

LOVE
&
SUPPORTS

Friendship

BFF

Besties
for the
Resties

STAY PAWSITIVE

Little Friends

41

Home sweet Home

Dream house

Cozy

Convenient

Peace   **Dream car**

Comfort   SAFE ZONE

Education

Reading

Focus

Learning

The more you practice,
the better you get.

NEVER GIVE UP

Live your
Dream

Graduation

Career

Master's Deegree

HARD-WORKING

Dream job

SUCCESSFUL DEVELOPMENT

START UP

Investment

Self-employed

Money

Saving

Financial freedom

MILLIONAIRE

DEBT FREE

Adventure Vacation

TRAVEL Just Go

EXPLORE

Beach life

Natural Life

ENGLAND

FRANCE

MEXICO

ITALY

JAPAN

AUSTRALIA

NETHERLANDS

IRELAND

VENICE

BALI

DUBAI

THAILAND

SOUTH AFRICA

CANADA

SPAIN

AAAAAABBBB
CCCCDDDDEE
EEEFFFFFGG
GGGHHHHHHI
IIIIIJJJJJKKKK
LLLLLMMMM
MNNNNNOOOO

PPPPPPQQQRR
RRRSSSSST
TTTTUUUUUV
VVWWWXX
XXYYYYYYYZ
ZZZ111122
2334444555

6667777888
999000!!!
??? , , . . " "
" " * * @ @ #
$ $ % % & & +
+ = = (( ))